W9-AOM-678

NATURE'S LIGHT SHOW

LIGHTNING

By Kristen Rajczak

 Gareth Stevens
Publishing

Please visit our website, www.garethstevens.com. For a free color catalog of all our high-quality books, call toll free 1-800-542-2595 or fax 1-877-542-2596.

Library of Congress Cataloging-in-Publication Data

Rajczak, Kristen.
Lightning / Kristen Rajczak.
        p. cm. — (Nature's light show)
Includes index.
ISBN 978-1-4339-7024-5 (pbk.)
ISBN 978-1-4339-7025-2 (6-pack)
ISBN 978-1-4339-7023-8 (library binding)
1. Lightning—Juvenile literature. I. Title.
QC966.5.R35 2013
551.56'32—dc23

                                        2011045162

First Edition

Published in 2013 by
Gareth Stevens Publishing
111 East 14th Street, Suite 349
New York, NY 10003

Copyright © 2013 Gareth Stevens Publishing

Designer: Katelyn E. Reynolds
Editor: Kristen Rajczak

Photo credits: Cover, p. 1, (cover, pp. 1, 3–24 background) Samuel D. Barricklow/Workbook Stock/Getty Images; (cover, pp. 1, 3–24 graphics), pp. 4, 5, 12, 13, 16, 21 (main) Shutterstock.com; p. 7 Hemera/Thinkstock.com; p. 9 Ed Darack/Taxi/Getty Images; pp. 11, 21 (inset) Dorling Kindersley/Getty Images; p. 10 Insa Korth/AFP/Getty Images; p. 14 Eastview/Wikipedia; p. 15 Jim Corwin/Photo Researchers/Getty Images; p. 17 John Grainger/Newspix/Getty Images; pp. 19, 20 iStockphoto/Thinkstock.com.

Printed in the United States of America

CPSIA compliance information: Batch #CS12GS: For further information contact Gareth Stevens, New York, New York at 1-800-542-2595.

CONTENTS

Words in the glossary appear in **bold** type the first time they are used in the text.

BRIGHT LIGHTNING

Have you ever seen the sky light up during a rainstorm? You've seen lightning! A bolt of lightning is easy to miss since it happens so fast. It often looks like a crack in the sky or an uneven staircase.

Did you know that lightning is electricity? That's why it's so bright. However, while lightning is a beautiful part of nature, it's also dangerous and can cause fires, loss of power in homes, and even death.

Lightning can cause loss of power in homes and businesses by striking power lines.

Lightning can strike during snowstorms, dust storms, and after **volcanic eruptions**.

Lightning can strike the water! Fish swimming nearby can be killed by the electrical **charge**.

LIGHTNING AND THUNDER

Lightning occurs in every storm that has thunder. In fact, lightning causes thunder to happen! But what causes the thunderstorms that result in lightning and thunder?

Thunderstorms form when wet air meets dry air or when warm air meets cold air. The warm air rises and cools. As it cools, **water vapor** in the air **condenses** and creates a cloud. The cloud keeps rising, and drops of water and ice form inside it. Rain or snow may begin to fall from these clouds.

EYE ON THE SKY

When lightning strikes, it heats the air and causes it to **expand** quickly. This produces the sound we call thunder.

A bolt of lightning is also called a stroke.

ELECTRIFIED!

Inside the thundercloud, drops of water, hail, and snow move around and run into each other. This causes them to become charged. Lighter drops of water and ice crystals gain a positive charge. Heavier ones gain a negative charge.

Negative charges gather in the middle of the cloud. Positive charges gather above and below the negatively charged area. Lightning is the electricity released when it becomes impossible for air to keep the charged areas apart.

EYE ON THE SKY

Positive and negative charges **attract** each other. As charges build up in a cloud, their attraction does, too.

This picture shows lightning striking the coast of Florida. Florida has the most lightning activity of any US state.

9

LIGHTNING AT GROUND LEVEL

Some lightning never leaves the clouds. However, some lightning strikes buildings, boats, or the ground!

As a cloud's electrical charges build up, the ground below the cloud also gains a charge. The charge on the ground is the opposite of the charge at the bottom of the cloud. The ground's charge is greater in tall objects, like mountains and trees. These charges attract the cloud's charge. Then, electricity travels between them as lightning!

▲ This wind turbine lost a blade after being struck by lightning.

This illustration shows the lightning caused by the attraction between the negatively charged cloud and positively charged ground.

EYE ON THE SKY

While it's more likely for lightning to strike something tall, lightning can strike anything. It's hard to guess what path a lightning stroke will travel.

LIGHTNING AROUND THE WORLD

Lightning occurs most often during seasons when thunderstorms are common. In the Northern **Hemisphere**, many thunderstorms occur between May and September. They are most common between November and March in the Southern Hemisphere.

The Democratic Republic of Congo in central Africa experiences the most lightning anywhere in the world. Warm, wet ocean air meets the cooler air of the country's mountains, causing year-round storms that produce lightning.

Africa

Democratic
Republic
of Congo

People sometimes say lightning never strikes in the same place twice, but that's not true. In fact, the Empire State Building in New York City is struck more than 100 times each year.

Lightning can cause a lot of harm. It can even split open big trees like this one!

TYPES OF LIGHTNING

Sometimes lightning **reflects** off clouds, lighting them up. That's called sheet or heat lightning. Which kind it is depends on where you are. If you're close enough to hear thunder, you've seen sheet lightning. If you're too far away to hear thunder, you'll call it heat lightning.

A red sprite is red lightning that happens above storm clouds and can be miles long. A blue jet is cone-shaped lightning that glows blue. It happens above a storm's center and then travels up very quickly.

A large red sprite like this one may actually be a group of red sprites packed tightly together.

When lightning strikes at night, it lights up the sky!

EYE ON THE SKY

Lightning sometimes forms a round glowing ball called ball lightning. Some balls are as small as a golf ball. Others are beach-ball size!

15

LIGHTNING FAST!

Lightning is a powerful force of nature. It's **destructive** and deadly. Each lightning bolt can contain as many as 1 billion **volts** of electricity! It can heat the air around itself to five times hotter than the surface of the sun.

Lightning can travel about 62,000 miles (99,760 km) per second. It's so fast we often can't tell when many lightning strokes have hit the same spot. To us, it just looks like one flickering lightning stroke.

Lightning strikes in southern Wyoming in 2004.

Lightning is most likely to strike during the summer. However, it can happen at any time of the year.

A house in Queensland, Australia, catches fire after being struck by lightning.

WHEN LIGHTNING STRIKES

Each year, thousands of people around the world are struck by lightning. About 100 die every year in the United States alone. When struck by lightning, a person's heart may stop beating.

Survivors often have serious health problems long after being struck by lightning. In addition to burns, they may experience memory loss, problems with their lungs and other body parts, or trouble sleeping. It's important for someone struck by lightning to get medical help immediately.

EYE ON THE SKY

Many people aren't directly struck by lightning. They are struck by the electricity moving along the ground.

According to the National Weather Service, about 300 people report injuries caused by lightning every year.

19

LIGHTNING SAFETY

When a thunderstorm hits, there's always a chance lightning will strike. Go inside as soon as you hear thunder or see lightning. Houses, malls, and other strong buildings are the safest places to be. Once inside, stay away from electronics, such as computers and TVs, as well as sinks and showers. They're all pathways through which electricity could travel.

If you can't go indoors, stay away from trees. Put your feet close together and crouch, keeping your body close to the ground without touching it more than you must.

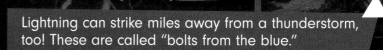

Lightning can strike miles away from a thunderstorm, too! These are called "bolts from the blue."

HOW LIGHTNING FORMS

1. A storm cloud forms.

2. Water, ice, or hail moves around inside the cloud. Water drops or ice crystals become charged when they run into each other.

3. Negatively charged drops or ice crystals fall to the bottom of the cloud. Positively charged drops or crystals rise to the top of the cloud.

4. The charges attract each other, releasing electricity.

5. The ground becomes charged. Lightning hits!

GLOSSARY

attract: to draw toward

charge: to become electrified. Also, the electricity in something.

condense: to change from a gas to a liquid

destructive: able to cause damage

expand: to spread out

hemisphere: one of the halves of Earth. The equator divides Earth into the Northern and Southern Hemispheres.

reflect: to bounce off something

volcanic eruption: the bursting forth of hot, liquid rock from within Earth

volt: a measurement of the force that moves electricity

water vapor: water in the form of a gas

FOR MORE INFORMATION

Books

Bodden, Valerie. *Thunderstorms*. Mankato, MN: Creative Education, 2012.

Davids, Stacy B. *Strange but True Weather*. Mankato, MN: Capstone Press, 2011.

Fleisher, Paul. *Lightning, Hurricanes, and Blizzards: The Science of Storms*. Minneapolis, MN: Lerner Publications, 2011.

Websites

Lightning
www.weatherwizkids.com/weather-lightning.htm
Read the answers to common questions about lightning.

Lightning: The Shocking Story
www.nationalgeographic.com/features/96/lightning/
Learn more about lightning, and read stories from survivors of lightning strikes.

INDEX